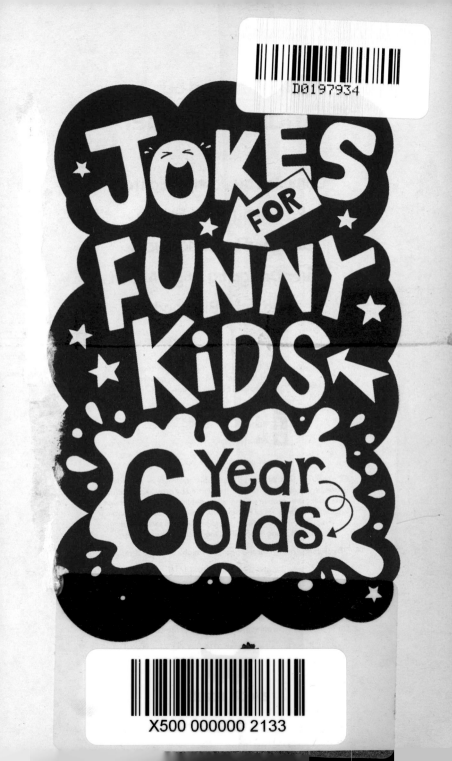

JOKES FOR FUNNY KIDS

6 Year Olds

Illustrated by
Andrew Pinder

Compiled by Jonny Leighton

Edited by Helen Brown

Designed by Jack Clucas

Cover Design by Angie Allison

and John Bigwood

First published in Great Britain in 2019 by Buster Books,
an imprint of Michael O'Mara Books Limited,
9 Lion Yard, Tremadoc Road, London SW4 7NQ

W www.mombooks.com/buster

f Buster Books

y @BusterBooks

A CIP catalogue record for this book is available from the British Library.

ISBN: 978-1-78055-626-0

2 4 6 8 10 9 7 5 3 1

Papers used by Buster Books are natural, recyclable products
made from wood grown in sustainable forests. The manufacturing processes
conform to the environmental regulations of the country of origin.

Printed and bound in August 2019 by CPI Group (UK) Ltd,
108 Beddington Lane, Croydon, CR0 4YY, United Kingdom

MIX
Paper from
responsible sources
FSC® C020471
FSC
www.fsc.org

CONTENTS

Introduction

Why do you like jokes about eggs?

Because they
crack you up.

Welcome to this te he he-larious collection
of the best jokes for 6-year-olds.

In this book you will find over 300 egg-cellent
jokes which will have you cracking up with
laughter – from silly space and amusing animals
to marvellous monsters and funny food.

If these jokes don't tickle your funny bone
then nothing will. Don't forget to share your
favourites with your friends and family
and practise your comic timing!

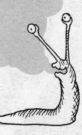

Spooky and Kooky

What do ghosts have for lunch?

I-scream on toast.

What do you give a ghost with bad eyesight?

Spook-tacles.

Which football position do ghosts like to play in?

Ghoul-keeper.

What do you call a crime-fighting ghost?

A police in-spectre.

What do ghost pandas eat?

Bam-BOO!

What are ghosts most afraid of?

Public spooking.

Why didn't the skeleton go to the party?

They had no-body to go with.

What's a skeleton's favourite musical instrument?

A trom-bone.

What do you call a skeleton that won't get up in the morning?

Lazy bones.

What does a skeleton order at a restaurant?

Spare ribs.

How did the skeleton know it was going to snow?

He could feel it in his bones.

What do you call a skeleton who goes out in the snow?

A numb-skull.

What do you call a witch on a beach holiday?

A sand witch.

What's the problem with twin witches?

You never know which witch is which.

What do witches race on?

VROOM-sticks.

What's a witch's favourite school subject?

Spelling.

What kind of tests do witches do at school?

Hex-ams.

What do you call two witches who live together?

B-room mates.

What's a zombie's favourite type of weather?

Cloudy with a chance of brain.

When do zombies sleep?

When they are dead tired.

What's a zombie's favourite meal?

You! Run away, now!

How do you say goodbye to a vampire?

See ya later, sucker!

What's a vampire's favourite type of dog?

A bloodhound.

Why do vampires need mouthwash?

They've got bat breath.

Why did the monster eat the tightrope performer?

He wanted a balanced diet.

What time is it when a huge monster sits on your house?

Time to get a new house.

What do you call a werewolf with no legs?

Anything you like, it can't catch you!

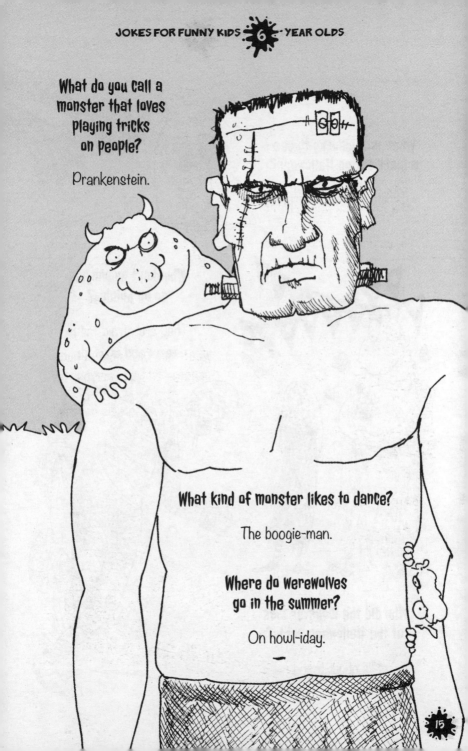

What do you call a monster that loves playing tricks on people?

Prankenstein.

What kind of monster likes to dance?

The boogie-man.

Where do werewolves go in the summer?

On howl-iday.

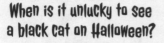

When is it unlucky to see a black cat on Halloween?

When you're a mouse.

Why don't mummyies go on holiday?

They are afraid they'll relax and unwind.

Who did the monster kiss at the Halloween party?

His ghoul-friend.

Why is it safe to tell a mummy your secrets?

Because they will always keep them under wraps.

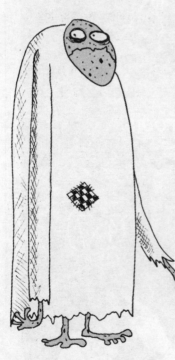

What do you do with a green monster?

Wait until it's ripe.

Why was the boy upset to win best Halloween costume?

Because he wasn't even wearing a mask.

School Drools

**What kind of school
do pilots go to?**

High school.

**What kind of school
do surfers go to?**

Boarding school.

**Why do magicians
make great teachers?**

They're always asking
trick questions.

What's the difference
between a swamp
and school gravy?

Sadly, not a lot.

How do elves
learn to spell?

They use the elf-abet.

What object is the
king of the classroom?

The ruler.

What's the best way to get straight As?

Use a ruler!

What do you call a teacher in a rush?

A Russian teacher.

Pupil: I didn't deserve zero out of ten on the last test.

Teacher: I agree, but it was the lowest mark I could give you.

Why does my teacher wear sunglasses?

Because I'm so bright.

What do gnomes do after school?

Gnome-work.

What's a snake's favourite lesson?

Hissss-tory.

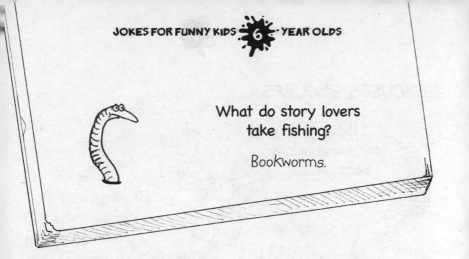

What do story lovers
take fishing?

Bookworms.

Why did the music
teacher carry a ladder
around with him?

To reach the
high notes.

Teacher: Why
are you late?

Pupil: I'm not late, I'm
EARLY for tomorrow!

EXCUSES, EXCUSES ...

I didn't do
my homework
because ...

The dog ate it.
(He said it was
delicious.)

My dad put it in the
washing machine. At
least it's clean ...

I was
abducted
by aliens. And
they didn't know
the answers either.

It got struck by lightning.

A gust of wind blew it out of the window.

I'm allergic to maths. It makes me all itchy.

How does a bee get to school?

It takes the buzz.

Why are fish so clever?

Because they are always in schools.

Why was the Viking ship so cheap?

It was on sail.

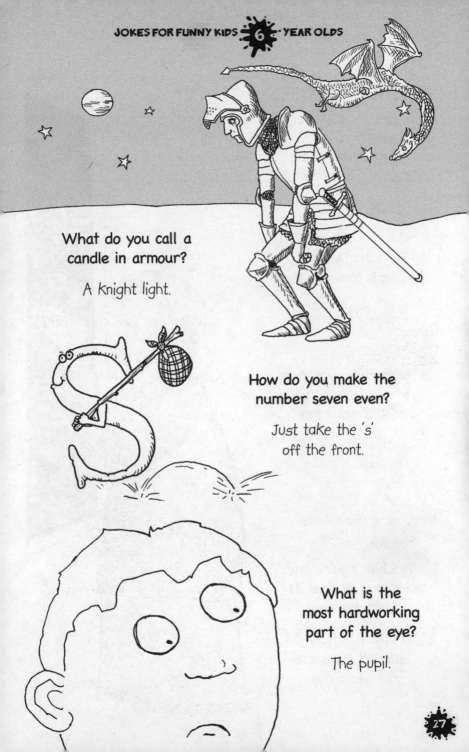

What do you call a candle in armour?

A knight light.

How do you make the number seven even?

Just take the 's' off the front.

What is the most hardworking part of the eye?

The pupil.

EXCUSES, EXCUSES ...

Teacher: Why are you late for school?

Pupil: My mum's car broke down.

Teacher: Don't you walk to school?

Teacher: Do you even know the meaning of the word late?

Pupil: No – maybe you could teach me?

Teacher: You're late. History started 10 minutes ago.

Pupil: I thought it started thousands of years ago.

Teacher: You're late. Don't you have a watch?

Pupil: I threw it out the window so time would fly.

Teacher: You're late again.

Pupil: You mean I have to be on time every day?

Teacher: What's your excuse this time?

Pupil: My shoes got a puncture.

Out Of This World

**Why did the alien
go to the doctor?**

It looked a little green.

**What do you get when
you cross an alien with
something white
and fluffy?**

A martian-mallow.

**What do Martians serve
their dinner on?**

Flying saucers.

Why did the star go to school?

To get brighter.

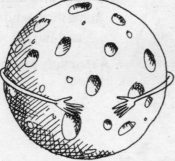

How do you know when the Moon has had enough to eat?

When it's a full Moon.

Why did the cow go into space?

To see the Mooooo-n.

What do planets like to read?

Comet books.

What's an astronaut's favourite key on the keyboard?

The space bar.

What do you call an alien starship that weeps?

A crying saucer.

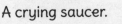

Which planet is the most bling?

Saturn, because it has rings.

Why was the restaurant on the Moon empty?

Because it had no atmosphere.

What happened when the girl stayed up all night looking for the Sun?

It suddenly dawned on her.

What did Earth say to the other planets?

You guys have no life.

What did the alien say to your gardener?

Take me to your weeder.

What do aliens like to drink?

Gravi-tea.

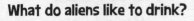

35

What do you get if you cross a wizard and an astronaut?

A flying sorcerer.

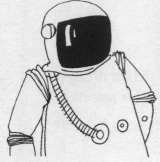

What do you call an alien with carrots in its ears?

Anything you want, it can't hear you!

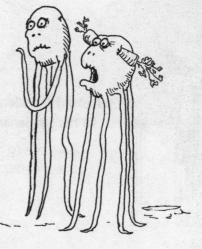

What kind of stars wear sunglasses?

Movie stars.

What did the astronaut find in his kitchen?

An Unidentified Frying Object.

What's an astronaut's favourite board game?

Moon-opoly.

What do astronauts spread on their toast?

Mars-malade.

What time do astronauts eat?

Launch time.

How do you get in touch with someone on Saturn?

Just give them a ring.

How does the Solar System keep its trousers up?

With an asteroid belt.

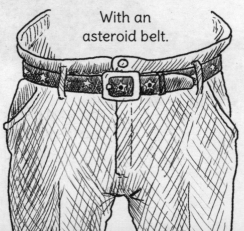

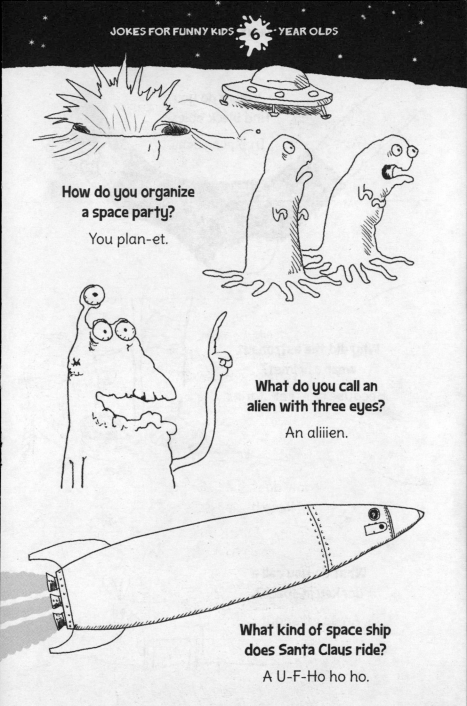

**How do you organize
a space party?**

You plan-et.

**What do you call an
alien with three eyes?**

An aliiien.

**What kind of space ship
does Santa Claus ride?**

A U-F-Ho ho ho.

**Where do you
find black holes?**

In black socks.

**Why did the astronaut
wear a helmet?**

Because her feet stank.

**What do you call a
donkey in space?**

An ass-tronaut.

What's a cow's favourite part of space?

The Milky Way.

Why did Mickey Mouse go into space?

He was looking for Pluto.

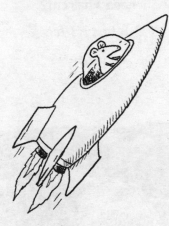

What did one alien say to the other?

It's nice to meteor.

What do you do if you see an alien in a crowd?

Give it some space.

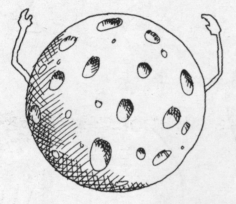

Why doesn't the Moon need a haircut?

It has no 'air.

Did you hear the joke about space?

It was too out of this world.

Comic Celebrations

What do you say to a kangaroo on its birthday?

Hoppy birthday!

Why do you put candles on top of a birthday cake?

It's too hard to put them on the bottom.

What does a snail do on its birthday?

Shell-abrate.

**What game do rabbits
play at birthday parties?**

Musical hares.

**What do you say to a
shark on its birthday?**

Have a fin-tastic day.

**What do you always
get on your birthday?**

Another year older.

Did you hear about the owl who didn't get any birthday presents?

It didn't give a hoot.

What goes up but never goes down?

Your age.

What does every birthday party end with?

The letter 'y'.

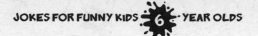

Why did the girl get heartburn from her birthday cake?

Because she left the candles on when she ate it.

Why didn't the teddy bear finish its birthday cake?

It was stuffed.

What does an elephant want for its birthdays?

A trunk-ful of presents.

What is the sneakiest Christmas treat?

Mince spies.

What do you call a naughty reindeer?

Rude-olph.

Why should you not start a fight with Santa?

Because he's got a black belt.

What do snowmen eat for breakfast?

Ice crispies.

What do monkeys sing at Christmas?

Jungle bells! Jungle bells!

What do you get if you eat Christmas decorations?

Tinsil-itus.

How does an elf get to Santa's workshop?

On his icicle.

What's the name of Father Christmas's dog?

Santa Paws.

What do you get if you deep fry a turkey?

Crisp-mas dinner.

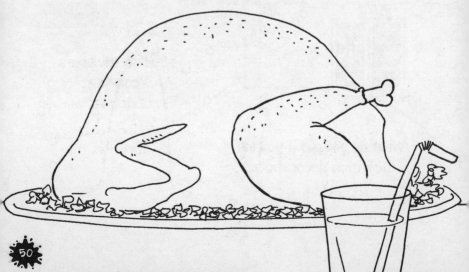

Knock Knock!

Who's there?

Arthur.

Arthur, who?

Arthur any mince pies left?

Who brings presents to sharks at Christmas?

Santa Jaws.

What do dinosaurs decorate at Christmas?

A Christmas Tree-Rex.

**What do sheep say
at Christmas time?**

Season's Bleat-ings.

**What's an elf's favourite
part of the school day?**

Snow and tell.

**What's an elf's favourite
type of music?**

Wrap.

What do you call Santa at the beach?

Sandy Claus.

What did one Christmas bauble say to the other?

I like hanging with you.

What kind of ball doesn't bounce?

A snowball.

What's a cow's favourite day of the year?

Moo Year's Day.

What do you say to a pirate on New Year?

Happy New Yarrrghh.

Why should you never climb aboard an alien spaceship on your birthday?

Because you might get carried away.

Why don't eggs tell jokes?

They might crack up.

What did the egg say to his friend?

Heard any good yolks lately?

How does the Easter Bunny stay fit?

Eggs-ercise.

Sporty Laughs

Why did the girl buy nine rackets?

Because ten-nis too many.

Why are football stadiums so cool?

They are full of fans.

Why are babies great at basketball?

They're always dribbling.

Why are boxers good at telling jokes?

They've got great punch-lines.

Why did the golfer wear two pairs of trousers?

In case they got a hole in one.

I thought I was getting better at skiing ...

... but lately I've been going downhill.

Why did the vampires cancel their baseball game?

They couldn't find their bats.

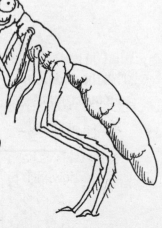

Which sport do insects love?

Cricket.

On what day are cheerleading ghosts most scary?

Fright-day.

What's a golfer's favourite drink?

Tee.

What do you call a girl in the middle of a tennis court?

Annette.

Why isn't Cinderella good at football?

She always runs away from the ball.

What's a runner's favourite school subject?

Jog-raphy.

What kind of exercise is best for a swimmer?

Pool ups.

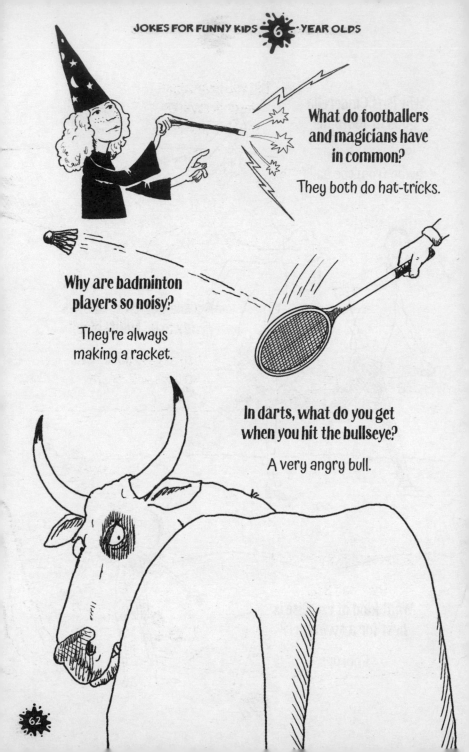

What do footballers
and magicians have
in common?

They both do hat-tricks.

Why are badminton
players so noisy?

They're always
making a racket.

In darts, what do you get
when you hit the bullseye?

A very angry bull.

Did you hear about the underwater snooker player?

He was a pool shark.

Why are elephants always ready to go swimming?

They always have their trunks with them.

Where do zombies go diving?

The Dead Sea.

Why did the football quit its team?

It was tired of being kicked around.

What should a football team do if the pitch gets flooded?

Bring on their subs.

Why are bicycles always falling over?

Because they're two tyred.

What's a runner's favourite vegetable?

Runner beans.

What did the baseball glove say to the ball?

Catch you later!

Why do fish hate tennis?

They don't like to get too close to the net.

**What do athletes
wear on cold days?**

Long jumpers.

**What's the hardest
part of ice skating?**

The ground.

**What's an insect's
favourite swimming stroke?**

The butterfly.

What do you call a man in a swimming pool?

Bob.

What's a footballer's favourite drink?

Penal-tea.

What's a waiter's favourite tennis shot?

The serve.

Why didn't the dog want to play football?

It was more of a boxer.

What's harder to catch the faster you run?

Your breath.

What kind of stories do basketballers tell?

Tall tales.

Animal Roarers

**Why did the
chicken cross the
playground?**

To get to the
other slide.

**What does a cat say
when it gets hurt?**

Me-owww.

**How does a lion
like its steak?**

ROAR!

Knock Knock!

Who's there?

Amos.

Amos, who?

Amos-quito!

Knock Knock!

Who's there?

Anna.

Anna, who?

Anna-ther mosquito!

**What colour
do cats love?**

Purrrr-ple.

What happened to the elephant who ran away with the circus?

He packed his trunk and left.

What do cows like to do on a weekend?

Watch moo-vies.

And where do cows watch them?

MooTube.

**What do you call a fly
without wings?**

A walk.

**What has eight arms
and tells the time?**

A clock-topus.

**How do snails keep
their shells shiny?**

Snail varnish.

What do you call a cat in the desert?

Sandy Claws.

Why did the octopus beat the shark in a fight?

Because it was well-armed.

What do you call a bear with no teeth?

A gummy bear.

My cat was just sick on the carpet ...

... I don't think it was feline well.

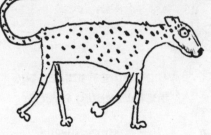

Why did the lion lose the race?

Because he was racing a cheetah.

Why are frogs so happy?

They eat whatever bugs them.

How many tickles does it take to make an octopus laugh?

Ten-tickles.

What animal makes the best chimney sweep?

A chimney sheep.

Why are dalmatians so terrible at hiding?

They're always spotted.

What do you call a fish with no eyes?

A fsh.

Which animals are always stealing things?

Crook-odiles.

What do you call a pig that does karate?

A pork chop.

**What do you call
a sleeping bull?**

A bulldozer.

**Where do rabbits
go after they
get married?**

On their bunny-moon.

**What do you call
a lazy kangaroo?**

A pouch potato.

Why did the snake cross the road?

To get to the other sssssside.

What do you call a lion's reflection?

A copycat.

What's black and white and delivers milk?

A panda with a milk round.

What does a spider do
when it gets angry?

It goes up the wall.

Why do lobsters
not give to charity?

They're shellfish.

Why do French
people eat snails?

They don't like fast food.

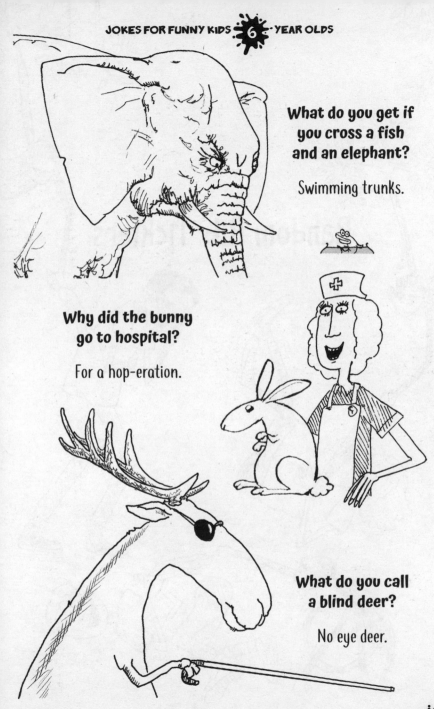

What do you get if you cross a fish and an elephant?

Swimming trunks.

Why did the bunny go to hospital?

For a hop-eration.

What do you call a blind deer?

No eye deer.

Random Rib Ticklers

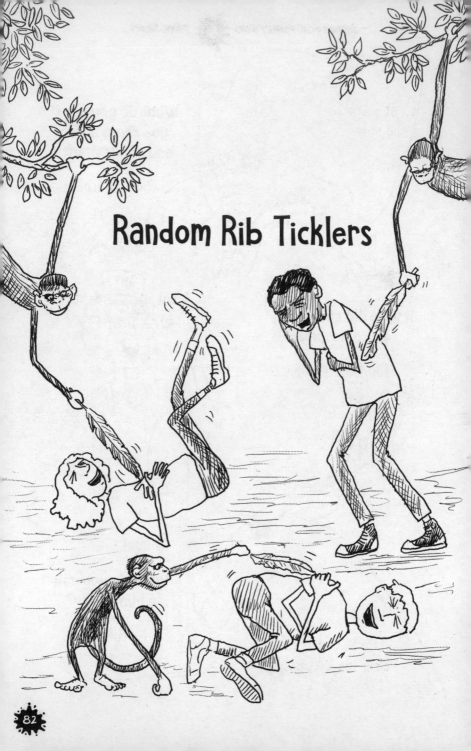

What's brown
and sticky?

A stick.

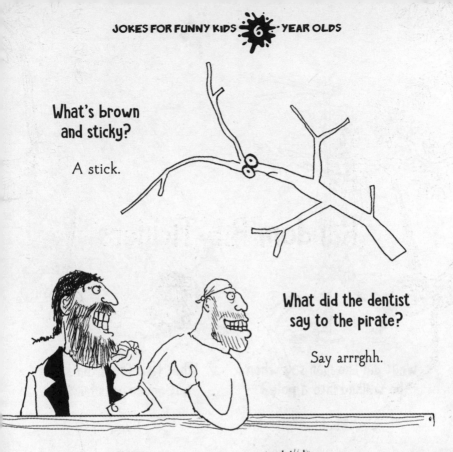

What did the dentist
say to the pirate?

Say arrrghh.

Knock Knock!

Who's there?

A little boy.

A little boy, who?

A little boy who can't
reach the doorbell!

What did the man say when he walked into a pole?

Ouch!

What falls from the sky but never gets hurt?

Rain.

What do you call cheese that isn't yours?

Nacho cheese.

What's orange and
sounds like a parrot?

A carrot.

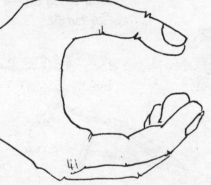

What did the finger
say to the thumb?

I'm in glove with you.

Why did the little boy
throw the toast out
of the window?

He wanted to see
the butter-fly.

What do you call a girl
with one leg shorter
than the other?

Eileen.

I used to be afraid
of hurdles ...

... but I got over it.

How do trees
make friends?

They branch out.

Don't you feel sorry for shopping trolleys?

They're always getting pushed around.

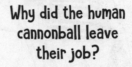

Why did the human cannonball leave their job?

They got fired.

What do clouds have on under their clothes?

Thunder-wear.

What kind of coat is wet when you put it on?

A coat of paint.

Why are pirates pirates?

Just because they arrrghh.

Why was 6 afraid of 7?

Because 7 ate 9.

What did one snowman say to the other?

Can you smell carrots?

Two fish are in a tank ...

... one says to the other, "I have no idea how to drive this thing".

Why don't monsters eat clowns?

Because they taste funny.

Knock Knock!

Who's there?

Cows go.

Cows go, who?

No silly, cows go moo!

What did the the doctor say to the boy with chocolate hanging out of his nose?

I don't think you're eating properly.

What's small, purple and dangerous?

A grape with a water pistol.

**What did the duck
ask for at the end
of a meal?**

The bill.

**Which side of a leopard
has the most spots?**

The outside.

**What's the difference
between broccoli
and bogeys?**

Children don't like
eating broccoli.

What do you call a blind dinosaur?

Do-you-think-he-saw-us.

Where do generals keep their armies?

Up their sleevies.

How do fish weigh themselves?

They have scales.

Where do wolves go to make movies?

Howl-ywood.

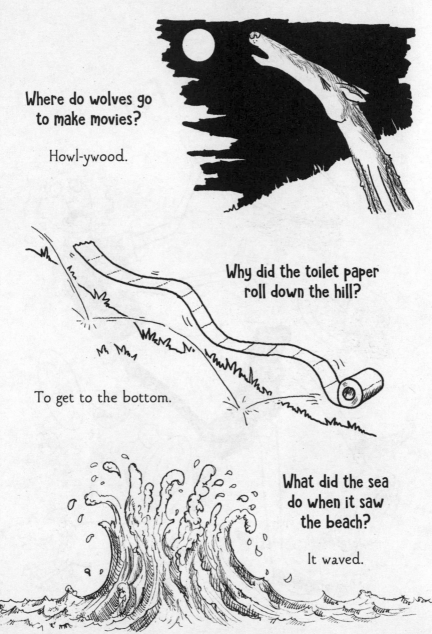

Why did the toilet paper roll down the hill?

To get to the bottom.

What did the sea do when it saw the beach?

It waved.

Foody Fun

What do you serve but never eat?

A tennis ball.

Why did the man get fired from the orange juice factory?

Because he couldn't concentrate.

Why is the sea so strong?

It has a lot of mussels.

Why did the biscuit cry?

Because his father
was a wafer so long.

I cut my finger chopping cheese ...

... but I think I have
grater problems.

Do you want to hear a joke about pizza?

Actually, never mind -
it's too cheesy.

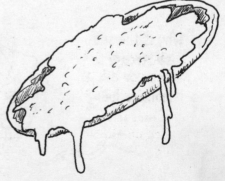

What's red and invisible?

No tomatoes.

Why did the tomato turn red?

Because it saw the salad dressing.

What do you get when you ask a lemon for help?

Lemon-aid.

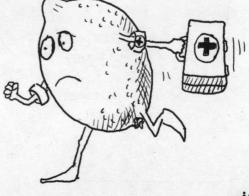

What do you call a fish with a tie?

So-fish-ticated.

What do you call a mischievous egg?

A practical yolker.

Did you hear the rumour about butter?

Sssh, don't spread it.

Why did the banana
go to the doctor?

It wasn't peeling well.

Cashew!

What kind of nut
always seems to
have a cold?

Cashew.

Which day of
the week do
eggs dread?

Fry-day.

Two muffins were in the oven. One said, "wow, it's hot in here."

The other said, "wow, a talking muffin."

What do sea monsters eat?

Fish and ships.

What cheese is made backwards?

Edam.

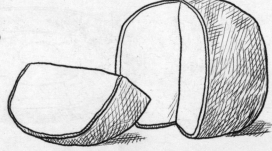

What do you get if
you cross a snake
and a pie?

A pie-thon.

What kind of
shoe can you make
from a banana?

A slipper.

What do cats eat
for breakfast?

Mice crispies.

What kind of key
opens a banana?

A mon-key.

Why did the pepper
put a jumper on?

It was a little chilli.

What do dogs eat
at the movies?

Pup-corn.

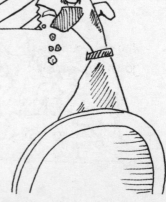

What did one plate say to the other plate?

Dinner is on me.

What do computers love to eat?

Micro chips.

Why did the biscuit go to the doctor?

Because it felt crumb-y.

What does bread
do on its day off?

Loaf around.

Why did the carrot like to
hang out with the mushroom?

He was a fun-guy.

What vegetables
do sailors hate?

Leeks.

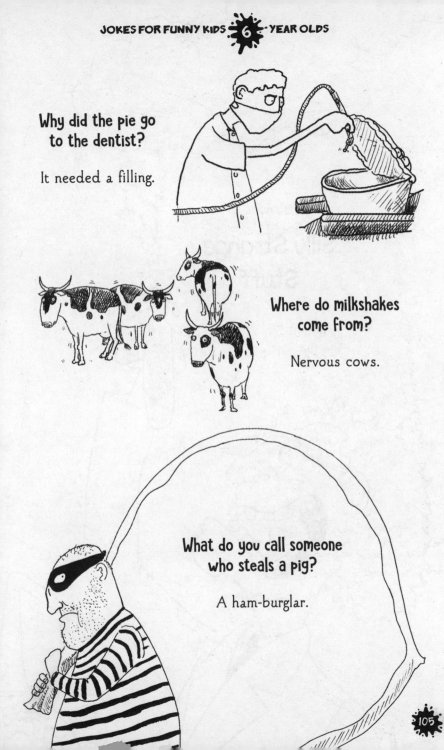

Why did the pie go
to the dentist?

It needed a filling.

Where do milkshakes
come from?

Nervous cows.

What do you call someone
who steals a pig?

A ham-burglar.

Silly Strange Stuff

What kind of androids do you get in the Arctic?

Snow-bots.

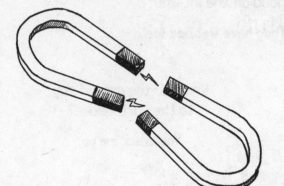

What did one magnet say to the other?

I find you very attractive.

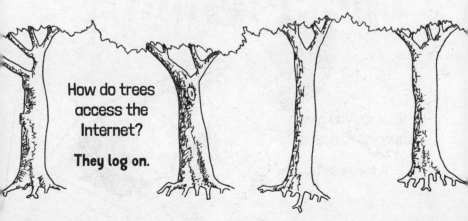

How do trees access the Internet?

They log on.

Why are penguins so good on the Internet?

They have webbed feet.

What did the ground say to the earthquake?

You crack me up.

What do you give a hungry computer?

A mega-byte.

What did one romantic volcano say to the other?

I lava you.

What is the centre of gravity?

The letter V.

Why can't a T–Rex clap?

Because it is extinct.

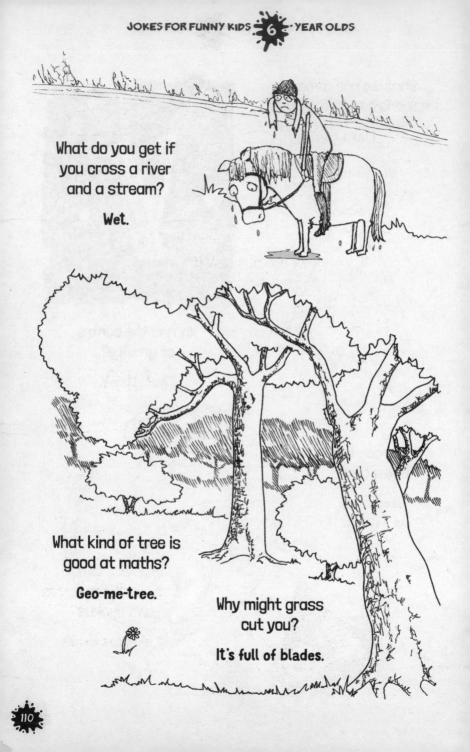

What do you get if you cross a river and a stream?

Wet.

What kind of tree is good at maths?

Geo-me-tree.

Why might grass cut you?

It's full of blades.

Why do toadstools grow so closely together?

They don't need mushroom.

How do you know if the sea's friendly?

Say "hello" and it'll wave back.

What lies at the bottom of the ocean and shakes?

A nervous wreck.

Where does a river
put its money?

In the river bank.

Which insect runs away
from everything?

A flea.

What's a robot's
favourite music?

Heavy metal.

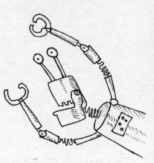

What do you say
to a dead robot?

Rust in peace.

Why do bees hum?

**Because they forgot
the words.**

What do you call a
frog with no legs?

Un-hoppy.

If a tree could hug you ...

... it wood.

What has a bottom
at the top?

Your legs.

Why are worms
always so
frightened?

**They have
no backbone.**

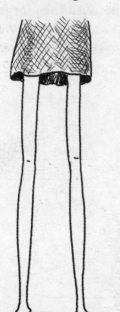

What's a tornado's
favourite game?

Twister

Why did the computer
keep sneezing?

It had a virus.

What do you get when
you cross a vampire
and a snowman?

Frost-bite.

How did the computer get out of prison?

It used the escape key.

Why would you take a laptop for a run?

To jog its memory.

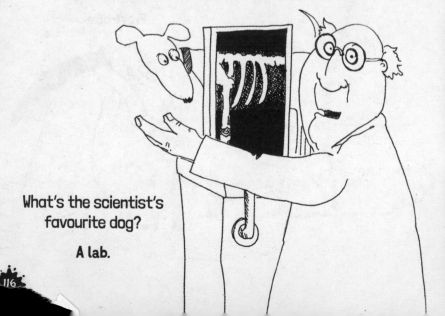

What's the scientist's favourite dog?

A lab.

What travels the
fastest – heat or cold?

**Heat – because you
can catch cold.**

Why did the
computer squeak?

**Someone stepped
on its mouse.**

Where do
dinosaurs
sunbathe?

At the dino-shore.

The Last Laughs

Knock knock!

Who's there?

Mice.

Mice, who?

Mice to meet you.

**Doctor, Doctor!
I think I've
swallowed a clock.**

Don't worry, it's no
cause for alarm.

**What do you call a man
with a toilet on his head?**

Lou.

Knock Knock!

Who's there?

Luke.

Luke, who?

Luke through the keyhole and you'll see.

What do you call a girl with a frog on her head?

Lily.

Doctor, Doctor! I feel like a violin.

Sit down while I make some notes.

Knock Knock!

Who's there?

Justin.

Justin, who?

Justin time for dinner.

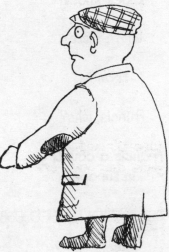

What do you call a man with no legs?

Neil.

Doctor, Doctor! I feel like everyone ignores me.

Next!

Knock Knock!

Who's there?

Francis.

Francis, who?

**Francis a country
in Europe.**

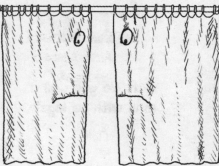

**Doctor, Doctor!
I feel like a pair
of curtains.**

Pull yourself together.

**What do you call a
man with a seagull
on his head?**

Cliff.

Knock Knock!

Who's there?

Lettuce.

Lettuce, who?

**Lettuce in —
we're freezing!**

**Doctor, Doctor!
I think I need
glasses.**

You definitely do.
This is the church.

**What do you call a
man with a spade
on his head?**

Doug.

Knock Knock!

Who's there?

Ice cream.

Ice cream, who?

Ice cream if you don't let me in.

What do you call a woman with slates on her head?

Ruth.

Doctor, Doctor! I feel like a deck of cards.

I'll deal with you later.

Knock Knock!

Who's there?

Orange.

Orange, who?

Orange you glad to see me?

Doctor, Doctor! I feel like a bee.

Buzz off!

What do you call a man with a cow on his head?

Pat.

Knock Knock!

Who's there?

Nun.

Nun, who?

Nun of your business.

What do you call a vicar on a scooter?

Rev.

Doctor, Doctor! I think I'm a bridge.

What's come over you?

Doctor, Doctor!
I feel like a cat.

How long have you
felt like this?

Ever since I
was a kitten.

What do you
call a woman with
holly on her head?

Carol.

Knock Knock!

Who's there?

A little old lady.

A little old lady, who?

I didn't know you
could yodel.

ALSO
AVAILABLE:

Jokes for Funny Kids:
8 Year Olds
ISBN: 978-1-78055-625-3

Jokes for Funny Kids:
7 Year Olds
ISBN: 978-1-78055-624-6